The BATHROOM GOLF COMPANION

———— • ————

by

Jack Kreismer

RED-LETTER PRESS, INC.
Saddle River, New Jersey

THE BATHROOM GOLF COMPANION
COPYRIGHT ©2013 Red-Letter Press, Inc.
ISBN-13: 978-1-60387-083-2
ISBN: 1-60387-083-0

Red-Letter Press, Inc.
P.O. Box 393
Saddle River, NJ 07458

www.Red-LetterPress.com

ACKNOWLEDGMENTS

EDITORIAL:
Jeff Kreismer

•

"HEAD" CONTRIBUTOR AND
LIFE OF THE POTTY:
Russ Edwards

•

BOOK DESIGN & TYPOGRAPHY:
Jeff Kreismer

•

COVER ART:
Cliff Behum

•

RESEARCH & DEVELOPMENT:
Kobus Reyneke
Mike Ryan
Mike Sauter

The
BATHROOM
GOLF
COMPANION

TEEING OFF

1. Who was the first to break 60 in a professional round of golf?

2. How about the first woman to do so?

3. Who was the first player to break 70 on all four rounds in the U.S. Open?

4. Can you name the first foreign golfer to win the PGA Player of the Year Award?

5. Who was the first lefty to win a major?

ANSWERS: 1.Al Geiberger, who shot a 59 at the Danny Thomas-Memphis Classic in 1977 2.Annika Sorenstam, at the Moon Valley Country Club in Phoenix, Arizona, in March 2001 3.Lee Trevino, in 1968 4.Nick Faldo 5.Bob Charles, the 1963 British Open

There are three roads to ruin: women, gambling, and golf. The most pleasant is with women, the quickest is with gambling, but the surest is with golf.

-Andrew Perry

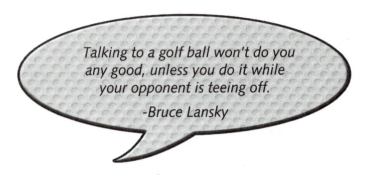

Talking to a golf ball won't do you any good, unless you do it while your opponent is teeing off.

-Bruce Lansky

There are 29 million golfers in the U.S., 77.5% of whom are male.

•

Bubba Watson is a member of the "Golf Boys," a band noted for its YouTube hit, "Oh Oh Oh."

•

Football Hall of Famer John Elway shot a hole in one on his 40th birthday.

•

Rory McIlroy provided early indication of golf potential when he hit a 40-yard drive at the age of two.

•

Canadian George Lyon won the Olympic gold medal for golf at the 1904 Games. Four years later when he came to defend his title, he found that everyone else had withdrawn. He was offered the gold medal by default, but refused- the only person to ever turn down the gold medal.

A pair of duffers await their turn on the tee, when a drop-dead gorgeous woman in her birthday suit runs across the fairway and into the woods. Two men in white coats, and another guy carrying two buckets of sand are chasing after her, and a little old man is bringing up the rear.

"What the heck is going on here?" one of the golfers asks the old geezer.

He says, "She's a nymphomaniac from the funny farm. She keeps trying to escape from the asylum and us attendants are trying to catch her."

The golfer says, "What about that guy with the buckets of sand?"

"Oh, him. That's his handicap. He caught her last time."

• • • •

And then there was the guy whose doctor advised him to play 36 holes a day so he went out and bought a harmonica.

What's nice about our Tour is you can't remember your bad shots.

-Bobby Brue, on the Senior PGA Tour

> *My golf game's gone off so much that when I went fishing a couple of weeks ago my first cast missed the lake.*
>
> *-Ben Crenshaw*

The longest golf course in the world is the par-72, 8,548 yard Jade Dragon Snow Mountain Golf Club in Lijiang, China. Its longest hole is the 711-yard, par-5 fifth.

•

Lori Garbacz added new meaning to the word "slice" on a golf course when she ordered a pizza at the 1989 U.S. Women's Open to protest slow play.

•

Too good to be true: The 1956 Tasmanian Open winner was a fellow named Peter Toogood. His father, Alfred Toogood, finished second and his brother, John Toogood, was third.

•

CBS sportscaster Jim Nantz and Fred Couples were teammates at the University of Houston.

To wash away the "evil lip-out curse," Mike Weir claims he puts his putter in the toilet the night before a tournament.

Nantz's No-No

Sportscaster Jim Nantz was on the air for a recap of the 2003 AT&T Pebble Beach National Pro-Am just after Davis Love had won the event. Joining him was guest celebrity Clint Eastwood.

Nantz thought he'd go ahead and make Clint's day when he remarked to Eastwood, "I'll bet you didn't know that when Davis was a young boy, one of the first adult films his father ever took him to see was one of yours."

Without missing a beat, Eastwood turned to Nantz and said, "I have never made an adult film in my life."

What a Card!

After a pro-am at Doral in 1970, Raymond Floyd wrote his front-side score of 36 in the space reserved for the ninth hole. He signed the card and ended up with a round of 110.

Mulligan: invented by an Irishman who wanted to hit one more twenty-yard grounder.

-Jim Bishop

> *I don't trust doctors. They are like golfers. Every one has a different answer to your problems.*
>
> -Seve Ballesteros

Bobo the Gorilla was making a fortune for his owner. They'd travel around to golf courses and challenge the local pro to a round. The pro would always take the bet, figuring he could easily beat the muscle-bound primate. That was, until Bobo stepped up to the tee and drove the ball 450 yards. That would usually be enough to scare off the pro, who'd be willing to settle the bet right then and there for a discounted sum of money.

One such morning, a top-rated pro conceded the bet after Bobo hit one of his monstrous drives. "Just out of curiosity," asked the pro, "how does Bobo putt?"

"The same as he drives...450 yards."

An alligator was celebrating his 25th year of guarding a water hazard at a South Florida course. When the club pro asked him what he would like in honor of the occasion, the gator replied, "You know, I've always wanted one of those shirts with a little picture of Arnold Palmer on the front."

PLAYING BY THE RULES
Are the situations listed below legal or illegal?

1. My driver breaks after hitting a ball during a match and I replace it.

2. I ask you what club you just hit.

3. My ball is overhanging the lip of the cup and I wait two minutes. At that point, the ball falls into the cup.

4. My ball is in the fairway and a loose twig is touching it. I pick up the twig and, in the process, my ball moves.

5. Just before putting, I use my club to flatten a few spike marks which are on my line.

ANSWERS: 1.Legal, if I don't delay play - However, if I've broken it in a fit of anger, I can't replace it. 2.Illegal - It's a two-stroke penalty for me, but if you answer me, you're slapped with the same. 3.Illegal – I'm assessed a one-stroke penalty. If it's my fourth shot, I get a five for the hole. 4.Illegal – The ruling calls for a one-stroke penalty. 5.Illegal - As a result, I am assessed a two-stroke penalty.

The way I putted, I must have been reading the greens in Spanish and putting them in English.

-Homero Blancas

> *I still enjoy the ooh's and aah's when I hit my drives. But I'm getting pretty tired of the aw's and uh's when I miss the putts.*
>
> *-John Daly*

Fred, playing as a single, was teamed with a twosome. Eventually, they asked why he was playing by himself on such a beautiful day.

"My dear wife and I played this course together for over thirty years but this year she passed away. I kept the tee time in her memory."

The twosome were touched at the thoughtfulness of the gesture but one asked him why no one from among her friends and family was willing to take her spot.

"Oh," responded Fred, "they're all at the funeral."

• • • •

A duffer lived a quarter mile from the local country club. One day he went into the pro shop and bought two dozen balls.

"You want these wrapped?" said the pro shop manager.

"Nah, I'll just drive them home."

LINGO OF THE LINKS

1. What's the modern-day name for the mashie?

2. What is an albatross?

3. What's the difference between match play and medal play?

4. You're my caddie as I play the back nine of the British Open. I ask for my jigger. What club do you hand me?

5. What does the phrase "through the green" mean?

ANSWERS: 1.The 5-iron 2.It's the British term for a double-eagle. 3.The winner at match play is determined by total holes won, while medal play is by total strokes. 4.The 4-iron 5.It means the entire golf course except the teeing ground, the putting green and all hazards. Out-of-bounds, of course, is not considered to be part of the course.

Hubert Green's swing looks like a drunk trying to find a keyhole in the dark.

-Jim Murray

> When I told the career guidance person
> I wanted to be a golf professional,
> he said that there's no such thing
> as a golf professional.
>
> -Bernhard Langer

In 1954, architect Robert Trent Jones received numerous gripes about the par-3 4th hole he had designed for the upcoming U.S. Open at Baltusrol. Jones decided to play it himself and recorded a hole-in-one.

•

The folks at Hillcrest Country Club in Beverly Hills once considered revoking the memberships of George Burns and Harpo Marx. The reason – they played a round of golf in their underwear.

•

A survey by the National Golf Foundation revealed that the typical amateur golfer averages a 97 for 18 holes. The average golfer's handicap is 15.1.

•

Jack Nicklaus and Nick Price share the record for the longest holed putt in a major tournament- 110 feet. Nicklaus made his record-setting putt in the 1964 Tournament of Champions and Price equaled it in the 1992 PGA Championship.

Military Mayhem

Lee Trevino once said that he played "World War II golf – out in 39 and back in 45." While that may get a chuckle, the folks at the St. Mellons Golf and Country Club in England were very serious about the war and posted the following rules:

Players are asked to collect bomb and shrapnel splinters found on the course.

In competition, during gunfire, or while bombs are falling, players may take shelter without penalty for ceasing play.

A ball moved by enemy action may be replaced, or if lost or destroyed, a ball may be dropped without penalty, not nearer the hole.

A player whose stroke is affected by the explosion of a bomb may play another ball under penalty of one stroke.

I didn't need to finish college to know what golf was all about. All you need to know is to hit the ball, find it and hit again until it disappears into the hole in the ground.

-Fuzzy Zoeller

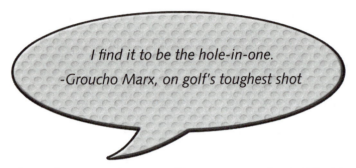

I find it to be the hole-in-one.

-Groucho Marx, on golf's toughest shot

A small private plane was flying over southwest Florida when all of a sudden the engine died, miles away from any airport.

The pilot turned to his wife and said, "Don't worry honey, there're dozens of golf courses in this area. I'll just land on the next one I see."

To which his wife replied, "What do you mean 'don't worry'? I've seen you play. You'll never hit the fairway!"

• • • •

Four old golfers took to the links on a Saturday morning as they had every week for the past ten years. The competition was as keen as ever.

On the sixth hole, one of the golfers suddenly collapsed just as he was about to hit a bunker shot. As he lay on the ground, one of the other golfers shouted, "I think Nellie just had a stroke."

Said another player, "Well, just make sure he marks it on his card."

Four old duffers had a Saturday morning 8 o'clock tee time for years. On one such morning, they noticed a guy watching them as they teed off. At every tee, he caught up with them and had to wait.

When they reached the fifth tee, the guy walked up to the foursome and handed them a card which read, "I am deaf and mute. May I play through?"

The old duffers were outraged and signaled to him that nobody plays through their group. He'd just have to bide his time.

On the eighth hole, one of the foursome was in the fairway lining up his second shot. All of the sudden he got bopped in the back of the head by the tremendous force of a golf ball. He turned around and looked back at the tee.

There stood the deaf mute, frantically waving his arm in the air, holding up four fingers.

Do pediatricians play miniature golf on Wednesdays?

-Jeff Kaye

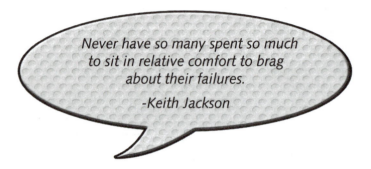

Never have so many spent so much to sit in relative comfort to brag about their failures.

-Keith Jackson

Harry loved golf more than anything but as he got into his 80's his eyesight began to fail him. Commiserating about his problem at the nineteenth hole, he met Louie, another octogenarian who lived for golf and, although he had perfect eyesight, was crippled by arthritis. They decided to join forces and play a round the next morning.

Harry teed off and the ball hooked a wee bit but landed not too far left of the green. "Hey, that felt good, Louie. Did you see where the ball went?"

"Sure did," replied Louie.

"So where'd it land?"

Louie scratched his head and replied, "I forget."

"Usually when I wake up in the middle of the night, it's to do something else."

–Tiger Woods, when asked if he ever wakes up at night to think about what he's accomplished in golf

THE ALMIGHTY DOLLAR

1. Who was the first golfer to exceed $10 million in career earnings?

2. In 1990, this merry player was the first to win a million dollars in a year on the Senior Tour. Who is he?

3. Who, in 2001, became the first LPGA player to top the $2 million mark with $2,105,868 in earnings?

4. True or False? In 1951, the legendary Babe Zaharias was the LPGA's top earner with just $15,087 in winnings.

5. Who tops the list of all-time money winners on the PGA Circuit?

ANSWERS: 1.Greg Norman 2.Lee Trevino 3.Annika Sorenstam 4.True 5.Tiger Woods

There's an old saying:
If a man comes home with sand in his
cuffs and cockleburs in his pants, don't
ask him what he shot.

-Sam Snead

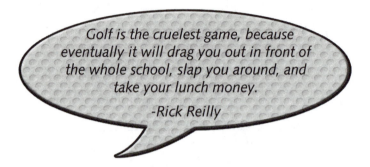

Golf is the cruelest game, because eventually it will drag you out in front of the whole school, slap you around, and take your lunch money.

-Rick Reilly

A guy was stranded on an island for ages. One day as he was walking on the beach, a beautiful woman in a wet suit emerges from the surf.

"Hey, cutie pie. Have you been here long?" she asks.

"I reckon about ten years."

"Do you smoke?"

"Oh, what I'd do for a cigarette!" he responds. With that, she unzips a pocket in the sleeve of her wet suit, pulls out a pack of cigarettes, lights one and gives it to him.

"I guess it's been a long while since you've had a drink, huh?"

"You got that right," he says.

She pulls out a flask from another pocket, gives it to him and he takes a swig.

"I bet you haven't played around in a while either," she coos as she begins to unzip the front of her wet suit.

Wide-eyed, he says, "Don't tell me you have a set of golf clubs in there too!?"

• • • •

According to the USGA, if your driver is out of line by one degree, the ball will be off target by ten yards.

•

In 1986, Wayne Grady was disqualified from both the Phoenix Open and the LA Open for hitting someone else's ball.

•

At the first Amateur Championship in 1895, the USGA ruled that Richard Peters would not be able to use his trusty putter- a pool cue.

•

Art Wall is credited with 46 holes-in-one, more than any other professional golfer in history.

> *Golf is just the old-fashioned pool hall moved outdoors, but with no chairs around the walls.*
>
> *-Will Rogers*

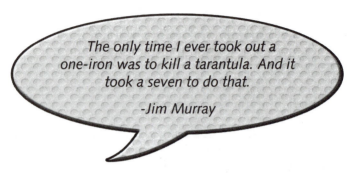

The only time I ever took out a one-iron was to kill a tarantula. And it took a seven to do that.

-Jim Murray

77-year old John Protti played a round of golf at the Vancouver Golf Club in 1994 after presenting a rain check dated April 7, 1948.

•

The Green Zone Golf Club is situated on the border of Finland and Sweden: nine holes are in one country and nine in the other.

•

A portrait of Bobby Jones that hangs at Augusta National Golf Club was painted by Dwight D. Eisenhower.

•

The U.S. Open was first televised in 1947, the British Open in 1955, and The Masters in 1956.

•

Sergio Garcia, who sank his first hole in one in 2012, has been coming up aces for a long time. Garcia's an avid poker player and has played on the Poker Stars tour.

•

The sand wedge was invented by Gene Sarazen in 1932.

WHO AM I?

1. I was from the small town of Pedrena, Spain, and I won three British Opens as well as two Masters.

2. I'm a dentist by trade but was pretty good at filling cavities on the golf course, too. I won the U.S. Open in 1949 as well as six other tournaments.

3. Joe DiMaggio's got nothing on me when it comes to streaks. I had 11 consecutive victories in 1945 when I had a total of 18 PGA Tour wins.

4. In 2013, I became the first Australian to win the Masters when I defeated Angel Cabrera in a two-hole playoff.

5. I was the first LPGA player to be named Rookie of the Year and Player of the Year simultaneously in 1978.

ANSWERS: 1.Seve Ballesteros 2.Cary Middlecoff 3.Byron Nelson 4.Adam Scott 5.Nancy Lopez

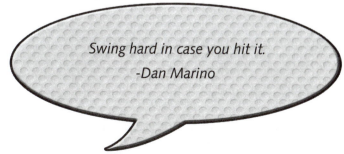

> *Every day I try to tell myself this is going to be fun today. I try to put myself in a great frame of mind before I go out - then I screw it up with the first shot.*
>
> *-Johnny Miller*

A married couple is out for their weekly round of golf. All is well until the 10th green. The Mrs. lines up her putt, but all of the sudden, she screams in agony and collapses.

The husband observes the calamity and shouts, "You're having a heart attack!"

His wife begs him, "Please, please help me, dear. Get a doctor, quick!"

The hubby races off to find help. Moments later, he returns to the green, picks up his putter and lines up his putt.

His wife can barely lift her head off the green as she glares at him and says, "I can't believe it. I'm dying here and you're putting!?"

"Calm down, hon," says the husband. "I found a doctor on the third hole and he'll be here to help you."

"How long will he be?"

"He should be here in no time at all," her hubby answers. "Everybody agreed to let him play through."

The golfer's ball landed in a thicket of weeds in the middle of some woods, an unplayable lie if ever there was one. He tried to line it up but realized it was futile so he picked the ball up and moved it to a better position, shouting to his playing partners, "Found it."

Suddenly, he had the feeling he was being watched. He turned around and saw an escaped convict whose picture had been plastered all over the newspaper. The two men looked at each other for a long moment, then the golfer whispered, "Shhhh. I won't tell if you don't."

Ticking Off The Golf Gods

Arnold Palmer lost the 1967 Bing Crosby Pro-Am by virtue of the fact that his tee shot on the 14th at Pebble Beach hit a tree and bounced out of bounds. He re-teed and tried again only to hit the same tree. Late that night, storm clouds gathered and a fierce Pacific gale uprooted the offending tree ensuring that it would never bother Arnie again.

Golf is the only sport where the object is to play as little as possible.

-Charles G. McLoughlin

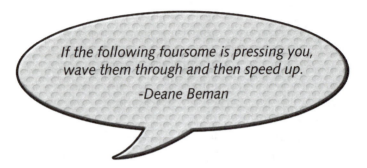

If the following foursome is pressing you, wave them through and then speed up.

-Deane Beman

In 2006, South Carolina's 12-year old Blake Hadden recorded two holes-in-one at the Future Masters. Hadden aced the 83-yard 5th hole and the 140-yard 11th hole at the Dothan Country Club in Alabama.

•

In 1973, Arthur Thompson shot a round of 103 at the Uplands Golf Course in British Columbia. Not bad for a man who was 103 years old.

•

The 365 acres that house the Augusta National Golf Club were purchased by Bobby Jones and fellow investors for $70,000 in 1931.

•

A golf cart is started and stopped an average of 150 times during a round of golf.

"The wind was so strong, there were whitecaps in the Porta-John."

–Joyce Kasmierski, at the 1983 Women's Kemper Open

Reel Tiger Tale

Tiger Woods and Mark O'Meara go way back as fishing buddies. O'Meara recalled the first time he ever went fishing with Tiger and asked him, "Have you ever thrown a big cast?" Tiger said, "Oh yeah, I can throw. Sure. No problem." With that, O'Meara said he took out his rod and gave it to Woods. Tiger let 'er fly and it was ... linguini!

• • • •

From the Golf Groaner Hall of Shame:

Q: Why is it so tough to drive a golf ball?

A: It doesn't have a steering wheel.

A guy in a golf cart yells to the slow-playing foursome ahead, "May I play through? My batteries are low!"

> *The ideal build for a golfer would be strong hands, big forearms, thin neck, big thighs, and a flat chest. He'd look like Popeye.*
>
> *-Gary Player*

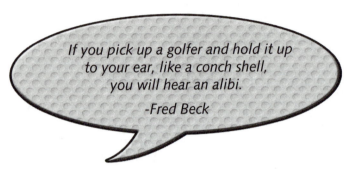

*If you pick up a golfer and hold it up
to your ear, like a conch shell,
you will hear an alibi.*

-Fred Beck

TRUE OR FALSE?

1. Charley Seaver, a member of the 1932 U.S. Walker Cup team, is the father of baseball great Tom Seaver.

2. Lee Trevino is one of a long line of golfers who attended the University of Texas.

3. Gary Player never won the PGA's Player of the Year award in his career.

4. Adam Scott is the great, great grandson of Clarence Scott, co-founder of the toilet paper manufacturing company that bears his name.

5. Byron Nelson led the 1943 U.S. Open going into the last round before it was called because of inclement weather.

ANSWERS: 1.True 2.False- Trevino never attended college. 3.True 4.False- but Clarence Scott is the co-founder of the company. He and his brother, E. Irvin Scott, began marketing the Scott paper product in 1907. 5.False- The Open was canceled that year because of World War II.

Dear Abby,

I've never written anything like this before, but I desperately need help. I think my wife's been unfaithful to me. She's been going out a lot lately- with "the girls" she says.

The "normal" routine is that one of her "girlfriends" picks her up before I get home from work. Even though I've tried to stay awake to see just who's dropping her off, I always fall asleep on the couch. Last night, though, I decided to do something a little different. I went down to the garage and hid behind my golf clubs so I could get a good view when she arrived home with her "girlfriend."

It was while I was crouched behind my clubs, that my dilemma came to light and I need your expert advice. I don't know whether this is a returnable deal or not, or whether I can remedy the problem myself- my driver has a hairline crack right near the club head!

Yours truly,

"Shafted"

I'm the worst golfer in the world and the worst singer in the world and I love both of those. Maybe I should sing while I'm playing golf.

-Jamie Farr

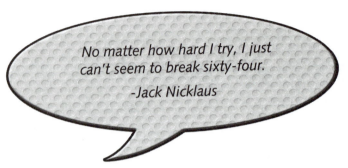

No matter how hard I try, I just can't seem to break sixty-four.

-Jack Nicklaus

In 1954, Laddie Lukas shot an 87 at the Sandy Lodge Golf Course in England - a decent performance, but it was really extraordinary considering what he was wearing – a blindfold.

•

After winning the 1949 L.A. Open, Lloyd Mangrum dropped his pants before the media to reveal why he won- lucky pajama bottoms!

•

Television did not impress Horton Smith, the president of the PGA Tour from 1952-54, who called it "a gimmick that wouldn't last."

•

Mr. Steven Ward shot a 222 at the 6,212-yard Pecos Course in Reeves County, Texas, on June 18, 1976. At the time, Mr. Ward was 3 years old.

•

Local rule at the Jinja Golf Course in Uganda: If a ball comes to rest in dangerous proximity to a crocodile, another ball may be dropped.

GIRL TALK

1. Who's affectionately known as "Big Mama"?

2. Who is said to have introduced golf to France?

3. She was the first woman to record an ace in USGA competition, making a hole-in-one during the 1959 U.S. Women's Open. (Big hint: A Hall of Famer, she's the all-time LPGA championship leader.) Name her.

4. The 2007 Kraft Nabisco Championship winner, at the age of 19, was the youngest ever to win an LPGA major tournament. Who is she?

5. Name the first native of India to join the LPGA tour.

ANSWERS: 1.JoAnne Carner 2.Mary, Queen of Scots ... The term "caddie" came to be as a result of Mary's use of actual cadets as her assistants. 3.Patty Berg 4.Morgan Pressel 5.Smriti Mehra, in 1997

> *I wish my name was Tom Kite.*
> *-Ian Baker-Finch, on signing autographs*

> *I'm hitting the woods just great, but I'm having a terrible time getting out of them.*
>
> -Harry Toscano

Fly Ball

Judy Rankin looked like she had the 1979, $150,000 LPGA Tournament locked up. She held a 5 shot lead after the 3rd round but then things started to slip. It all came down to a critical putt on the 17th. Just as she drew her putter back, a fly landed on the ball. Some deep reflex in Rankin's brain must have signaled swat because she whacked the ball so hard it went flying way past the hole, costing her the lead and the tournament.

• • • •

A very prominent CEO of a very big company was sent this ransom message: "If you ever want to see your wife again, bring $100,000 to the 16th green of Deerfield at eleven o'clock sharp tomorrow."

Well, the CEO didn't get there until noon. A masked man jumped out from behind some bushes and snarled, "What took you so long? You're an hour late."

"Hey, cut me some slack," said the CEO. "I have a twenty-five handicap."

A foreign spaceship hovered over a golf course and two aliens watched a lone duffer in amazement. The golfer hit his tee shot into the rough, took three shots to get back on the fairway, sliced the next one into the woods, and then took two to get back on the fairway again.

Meanwhile, one alien told the other that he must be playing some sort of weird game and they continued to watch in fascination.

The golfer then hit a shot into a bunker by the green. A few shots later, he made it onto the green. He four-putted to finally get into the hole.

At this juncture, the other alien said to his partner, "Wow! Now he's in serious trouble!"

Then there was the dyslexic duffer who always wondered how to flog.

Once when I was golfing in Georgia, I hooked the ball into the swamp. I went in after it and found an alligator wearing a shirt with a picture of a little golfer on it.

-Buddy Hackett

> *Golf is a dumb game. Hitting the ball is the fun part of it, but the fewer times you hit the ball, the more fun you have. Does this make any sense?*
>
> -Lou Graham

POTPOURRI

1. What is Chi Chi Rodriguez's real first name?

2. What LPGA player receives the Vare Trophy at the end of the year?

3. Can you name the golfing great who came up with the term yips to describe the tension afflicting a nervous putter?

4. What is the name of Augusta's minor league baseball team?

5. Name the only two men to win the U.S. Amateur, U.S. Open and U.S. Senior Open in their careers.

ANSWERS: 1.Juan 2.It's awarded to the player with the lowest scoring average for the year. 3.Tommy Armour 4.The Green Jackets 5.Arnold Palmer and Jack Nicklaus

The Bionic Invitational in Aiken, South Carolina, is open to all those who have had a joint surgically repaired.

•

Seve Ballesteros was disqualified from the 1980 U.S. Open after a traffic tie-up caused Ballesteros to arrive late at the first tee.

•

Survey Says: 7 out of 10 golfers claim they've either had their clubs stolen or know of someone who has.

•

Built in 1895, the Van Cortlandt Park Golf Course in the Bronx (N.Y.) was the first public golf course in the U.S.

•

Sam Snead's PGA Tour victories span a record 29 years, from his first win in 1936 to his last in 1965.

•

President Grover Cleveland decided against taking up golf in retirement, saying he was too fat.

Tranquilizers make it possible for a golfer to relax at his favorite form of relaxation.

-Stephen Baker

> *Golf was never meant to be an exact science- it's an art form. Einstein was a great scientist but a lousy golfer.*
>
> -Bob Toski

The Wrong Cup

Golf pro Homero Blancas was in the rough, carefully lined up his shot and then hit the ball. It bounced off a palm tree and landed in the bra of a spectator. Blancas conferred with Chi Chi Rodriguez as to what he should do and Rodriguez replied, "I think you should play it."

Presidential Pests

Richard Nixon may have had bugs and leaks but Dwight Eisenhower had a squirrel problem at the White House. The frisky critters were interfering with his putting practice on the lawn so he ordered them trapped and taken elsewhere. It wasn't as humane as you'd think. After all, where else but Washington, D.C. were the squirrels going to find as many nuts?

The 2013 Volvo World Match Play Championship in Bulgaria became one of golf's majors for potty jokes when Nicolas Colsaerts had to take a drop from the "nearest point of relief," a toilet in an outhouse (which had blocked his tee shot).

On a blistering day in south Florida, a priest, a minister and a rabbi were playing golf alongside beautiful Biscayne Bay. As the mercury climbed past 90, 95 and then topped 100 degrees, the men of cloth couldn't take it any longer. The bay looked so inviting that they decided to strip down and jump in the water.

After frolicking and splashing about for a while, they figured that they'd cooled down enough to get back to their game. Before they could dress, a foursome of lady golfers appeared nearby. The minister and priest covered their private parts in a panic but the rabbi just covered his face.

After the women passed by, the priest and minister asked the rabbi why he covered his face instead of his privates.

As the rabbi fastened the last button to his shirt, he replied, "Listen, I don't know about you, but in my congregation it's the face they'll recognize."

You know what I did at The Masters one year? I was so nervous I drank a fifth of rum before I played. I shot the happiest 83 of my life.

-Chi Chi Rodriguez

> *I play this game because my sole ambition is to do well enough to give it up.*
>
> -David Feherty

Tiger Woods goes into the nineteenth hole and spots Stevie Wonder. "Hey, Stevie, it's Tiger. How's your singing career doing these days?"

"I can't complain. How are you hitting 'em?"

Woods responds, "My swing is going real well right now."

Stevie says, "Mine, too."

"What? You play golf?" asks Tiger.

"Sure ... I've been playing for years," replies Stevie.

"But you're blind," Woods says. "How can you possibly play?"

Wonder replies, "I get my caddy to stand in the middle of the fairway and holler to me. When I hear the sound of his voice, I play the ball toward him. Then, after I get to where the ball lands, the caddy moves down to the green and again I play the ball toward his voice."

"But how do you putt?" asks Tiger.

"Simple ... My caddy lies down in front of the hole and calls to me with his head on the ground. And then I play the ball toward his voice," explains Stevie.

"What's your handicap, Stevie?"

Stevie responds, "I'm a scratch golfer."

Woods says, "We've got to play a round sometime."

"Sure, but people don't take me seriously, so I only play for money - and never for less than $5,000 a hole."

"You're on. When would you like to play?" asks Woods.

Stevie says, "Pick a night."

• • • •

Golf is what you play when you're too out of shape to play softball.

I'm trying as hard as I can, and sometimes things don't go your way, and that's the way things go.

-Tiger Woods

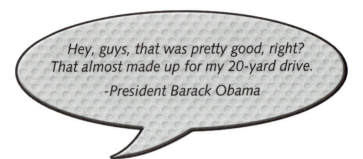

Hey, guys, that was pretty good, right? That almost made up for my 20-yard drive.

-President Barack Obama

POLITICALLY CORRECT

1. What president said, "A lot more people beat me now", when he was asked how his golf game changed after he left the oval office?

2. It was in San Francisco in 1925 when the first public golf course was named after a U.S. president. What was it called?

3. Fill in the blank: Comedian Bob Hope once quipped, "_____ made golf a contact sport."

4. What future president was once golfer Tommy Bolt's caddy?

5. Name the '60s chief executive who said, "I don't have a handicap. I'm all handicap."

ANSWERS: 1.Dwight Eisenhower 2.Harding Park, after President Warren G. Harding 3.Gerald Ford 4.Bill Clinton, at a tournament in Hot Springs, Arkansas 5.President Lyndon B. Johnson

The Puntas Arenas GC in Chile is the southernmost course in the world. Because of strong winds, the greens are set below the fairway level.

•

An Australian sponsor, a funeral director, once offered a prepaid funeral to anyone scoring an ace on a designated hole. Talk about a buried lie!

•

The Ryder Cup, now played in September, was originally held in June. In 1935, after the British complained of having to play in the heat of Ridgewood, N.J., a plan was worked out to move the match to a cooler month.

•

Ryo Ishikawa holds the record for the lowest score for a single round in a major pro golf tournament- 58 -at The Crowns of the Japan Golf Tour in Togo, Japan, in 2010. Ishikawa was 18 at the time.

Golf is the only game in which a precise knowledge of the rules can earn one a reputation for bad sportsmanship.

-Patrick Campbell

> *There would be nothing to get me to run for president. I don't even understand how anyone would want that job at all. Although I would be able to play golf, which I don't seem to have time now.*
>
> -Ellen DeGeneres

At a hoity toity country club which strictly enforces its rules, a member saw a guest of the club place his ball five inches in front of the tee markers.

The member hurriedly went over to the guest and said, "Sir, I don't know whether you've ever played here before, but we have very stringent rules about placing your tee at or behind the markers before driving the ball."

The guest looked the snooty club member right in the eye and retorted, "First, I've never played here before. Second," he added, "I don't care about your rules. And third, this is my second shot."

• • • •

A golf club walks into a bar and asks for a beer. The bartender refuses to serve him.

"Why not?" demands the golf club.

"Because you'll be driving later."

LAND OF THE LINKS

1. The Inverness Club was the site of two playoff losses by Greg Norman in the PGA Championship. Where is it?

2. What golf club hosted the first U.S. Open in 1895?

3. What Scottish course hosted the first twelve British Opens?

4. What famous seaside course was designed by amateur golfer Jack Neville in 1919?

5. Can you name the golf course which is named after a Dutch farmer who once owned the land?
(Hint: Jack Nicklaus won two of his four U.S. Opens there, in 1967 and 1980.)

ANSWERS:1.Toledo, Ohio 2.The Newport (Rhode Island) Golf Club 3.Prestwick Golf Club 4.Pebble Beach Golf Links in California 5.Baltusrol, in Springfield, New Jersey (The farmer's name was Baltus Roll.)

I played so bad, I got a get-well card from the IRS.

-Johnny Miller, on a miserable season

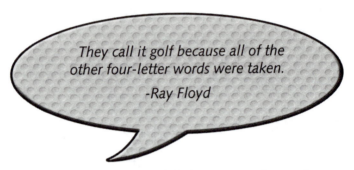

They call it golf because all of the other four-letter words were taken.

-Ray Floyd

Heading for the 19th hole? Experts say if you play a round of golf, then drink two cocktails, you've just gained more calories than you burned.

•

The first known women's tournament took place in Scotland in 1810. First prize was a fish basket.

•

The word "tee" comes from the Scottish term "teay" which is a small pile of sand. In days long gone by, golfers would make a teay and place the ball on top of it for driving.

•

Arnold Palmer's first PGA Tour check came at the 1955 Indiana Open. It was a modest $142.

•

Charles Sands of the United States won the first Olympic gold medal in men's golf at the 1900 Paris Olympics.

Who's The Real Goat Here?

At Florida's Sawgrass, Pete Dye got the idea to keep the weedy under-growth in the rough under control by using small herds of goats as they do in Ireland. The idea worked for a short time and then they had to buy mowers. Pete forgot that Ireland doesn't have alligators.

● ● ● ●

A duffer sliced his tee shot right into the woods. Rather than take a penalty, he decided to go for it. Unfortunately, his second shot caromed right off the trunk of a big old oak tree, hitting him right between the eyes and killing him instantly.

The next thing he knew, he was standing before St. Peter at the Pearly Gates. St. Peter, trying to find his name on the list, said, "Oh, here it is. But according to this, you're not scheduled to die for another 25 years. How did you get here?"

"In two."

I beat Tiger Woods by five strokes— but he was only six at the time.

-Kansas City Royals catcher Gregg Zaun

The difference between golf and the government is that in golf you can't improve your lie.

-George Deukmejian, former California Governor

A man went to a therapist for a consultation about an obsession that was ruining his health. "It's golf, Doc. Golf is destroying me. I'm desperate. I can't even escape it in my sleep. As soon as I close my eyes, I'm out there sinking a two-foot putt or making a magnificent drive right down the fairway. When I wake up in the morning, I'm even more tired than I was before I went to bed. What am I going to do? Can you help me?"

The therapist answered reassuringly, "First of all, you are going to have to make a conscious effort not to dream about golf. For example, when you close your eyes at night, try to imagine something else exciting, like discovering a gold mine or sailing on an around-the-world cruise."

The patient replied, "That's easy for you to say, Doc. If I do that, I'll miss my tee-time."

• • • •

Duffer: That can't be my ball. It's too old.

Caddy: It's been a long time since we teed off, sir.

Arguably the most famous left-handed golfer of all-time, Phil Mickelson is naturally right-handed.

•

In 2013, 77-year-old Gary Player became the oldest athlete ever to appear naked in the 'Body Issue' of "ESPN The Magazine."

•

Augusta's famed "Amen Corner" was coined by sportswriter Grantland Rice.

•

Arnold Palmer, the general of "Arnie's Army," served in the Coast Guard from 1951 to 1954.

•

The first time galleries were kept off the fairways and behind ropes at a tournament was in 1954 at the U.S. Open at Baltusrol Golf Club.

•

The maiden name of Jack Nicklaus's wife is Barbara Bush.

The only sure rule in golf is - he who has the fastest cart never has to play from a bad lie.

-Mickey Mantle

> *You know you're getting old when all the names in your black book have 'MD' after them.*
>
> -Arnold Palmer

WORDPLAY

See if you can identify the golf term from the high falootin' description given below.

Example: An "Aerodynamic Feathered Flyer" is the smartypants' way of saying "Birdie."

1. Concavity Covered Sphere

2. A Limb of the Vertebrate Family Canidae

3. Cross-Sectional Julienne

4. Hydrogen Dioxide Danger

5. Haliaeetus Leucocephalus

ANSWERS: 1.Golf Ball 2.Dogleg 3.Slice 4.Water Hazard 5.Eagle

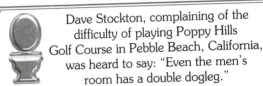

Dave Stockton, complaining of the difficulty of playing Poppy Hills Golf Course in Pebble Beach, California, was heard to say: "Even the men's room has a double dogleg."

Grave Consequences

Because the golf course in Tientsin, China, is laid out in a cemetery, greens are situated between grave mounds. Local rule: A ball which rolls into an open grave may be lifted without penalty.

• • • •

Two old golfers were reminiscing as they played. One pointed towards the woods. "My first girlfriend was named Mary Katherine Agnes Colleen Patricia Marion Margaret Kathleen O'Shaugnessey. Back when I was a lad, working as a caddie, I carved her name in one of those trees right over there."

"What ever happened?" asked his friend.

"The tree fell on me."

Groucho Marx said he was an ordinary fellow- "42 around the chest, 42 around the waist, 96 around the golf course."

Augusta National is the only course I know where you choke when you come in the gate.

-Lionel Hebert, on The Masters

> *A game in which one endeavors to control a ball with implements ill adapted for the purpose.*
>
> -President Woodrow Wilson

FOUR-LETTER MEN

The answers in this quiz all have four-letter last names.
Do you know...

1. The player who won The Heritage for the fifth time in 2003?

2. Who topped the 2006 senior money list and was named the Champions Tour Player of the Year as well?

3. Who won the 2013 U.S. Open, becoming the first English player to win a major since Nick Faldo in 1996?

4. The 2002 PGA champion?

5. The golfer whose first major win came at the age of 42 at the 1992 U.S. Open?

ANSWERS: 1.Davis Love III 2.Jay Haas 3.Justin Rose 4.Rich Beem 5.Tom Kite

Did you hear about the divorce lawyer who did a mailing to all the married male members of the exclusive country club?

She sent out 175 Valentines signed "Guess who?"

• • • •

Two golfers are standing on the 10th tee. Jerry takes about 20 practice swings, changes his grip five or six times, and adjusts his stance just as much.

"Hey, Jerry! Play, for heaven's sake. We don't have all day," says Larry.

"Hold on a minute, I gotta do this right. See the woman standing up there on the clubhouse porch? That's my mother-in-law and I would like to get off the perfect shot," says Jerry.

Larry looks, and about 250 yards away he sees the woman. "You must be kidding. You couldn't possibly hit her from here."

A Wisconsin man was cited for drunk driving after he crashed his golf cart into a highway road marker. The guy was driving his golf cart down the highway! Forget the drinking for a minute. How bad a golfer was this guy?

—Jay Leno

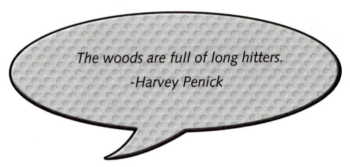

The woods are full of long hitters.

-Harvey Penick

Jack Nicklaus made his debut on the PGA Tour at the 1962 Los Angeles Open. He finished last in the money, earning $33.33.

•

In 1962, Australian meteorologist Nils Leid hit a golf ball 2,640 yards across the ice in Antarctica. That's approximately a one and a half mile tee shot!

•

The first British Open was originally called a "General Golf Tournament for Scotland" and was "open" to only eight invited professionals. It was played at Prestwick in 1860.

•

Against odds of 8,675,083 to 1, four golfers aced the 167-yard 6th hole at Oak Hill in Rochester, New York, during the same round of the 1989 U.S. Open: Mark Wiebe, Jerry Pate, Nick Price, and Doug Weaver.

•

Arnold Palmer broke 70 on the golf course before he hit the age of 12.

The Walker Cup was donated in 1921 by George Herbert Walker, President of the USGA in 1920, and grandfather of President George Herbert Walker Bush.

•

The first men-only golf clubs in the U.S. were nicknamed "Eveless Edens."

•

The Polo Golf Derby, played in Hempstead, Long Island, is for golfers and their carts. Players may only leave their carts while putting. It's all about hitting the ball without slowing down. The fastest time and the fewest strokes wins. Talk about being a good driver!

•

The youngest golfer to win the U.S. Open was Johnny McDermott, who was 19 years old when he won the title in 1911.

•

Presidents Truman, Ford, Bush (Sr.), and Clinton played golf right-handed but were natural lefties.

> *You never get golf. You play well one day, at least you play well for you, and you think you've got it. But you go out the next day and you haven't got it. Instead, it's got you.*
>
> *-John Madden*

> *If profanity had an influence on the flight of the ball, the game would be played far better than it is.*
>
> *-Horace Hutchinson, Hints on the Game of Golf, 1886*

SCREEN TEST

1. Adam Sandler portrays a hockey fanatic who discovers that he's a gifted golfer in this comedic 1996 flick. Do you know the title?

2. The wife of Archibald Leach has a starring role in "Caddyshack II". Can you name her? And, for extra credit, do you know her husband's stage name?

3. In the 1988 movie "Dead Solid Perfect", Kenny Lee's life on the pro tour presents more hazards than an entire season in the PGA. Who played him?

4. "Follow the Sun" starred Glenn Ford and Anne Baxter in a film about what golfing legend?

5. Do you know the TV sitcom character who won a Titleist hole-in-one award for hitting a ball into a whale's blowhole?

ANSWERS: 1."Happy Gilmore" 2.Dyan Cannon...Her husband was Cary Grant. 3.Randy Quaid 4.Ben Hogan 5."Seinfeld's" Kramer

LADIES' CHOICE

Test your knowledge of the Ladies Professional Golf Association.

1. Who was the first golfer to win all four LPGA majors in her career?

2. Who, in 2006, became the first woman to pass $20 million in LPGA Tour career earnings?
(Hint: She retired in '09.)

3. What was Babe Didrikson Zaharias' real first name?

4. She was the LPGA Player of the Year from 1966-'70 and from 1971-'73. Do you know her?

5. Of the thirteen original inductees into the World Golf Hall of Fame in 1974, two were women. Name them.

ANSWERS: 1.Pat Bradley 2.Annika Sorenstam 3.Mildred - as in Mildred Ella Zaharias 4.Kathy Whitworth 5.Patty Berg and Babe Didrikson Zaharias

I'm not an intellectual person. I don't get headaches from concentration. I get them from double bogeys.

-Tom Weiskopf

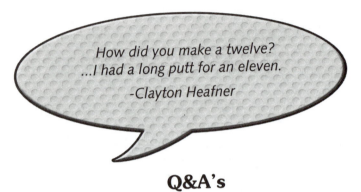

How did you make a twelve?
...I had a long putt for an eleven.
-Clayton Heafner

Q&A's

Q: How many golfers does it take to change a light bulb?
A: FORE!

Q: What did the Ancient Romans yell on the golf course?
A: "IV!"

Q: When is the course too wet to play?
A: When your golf cart capsizes.

Q: What is the easiest shot in golf?
A: Your fourth putt.

While Lee Trevino was on the PGA tour in 1968, he visited the Alamo, in San Antonio, Texas. Trevino exclaimed, "Well, I'm not gonna buy this place. It doesn't have indoor plumbing."

Q: How many golfers does it take to screw in a light bulb?

A: Two- One to do it and the other to tell him that he looked up.

Q: What type of engine do they use in golf carts?

A: Fore cylinder

Q: What do hackers and condemned playgrounds have in common?

A: Lousy swings

Q: How can you spot the golfers in church?

A: They're the ones who pray with the interlocking grip.

The difference between getting in a sand trap and getting in water is like the difference between an auto wreck and an airplane wreck. You can recover from one of them.

-Bobby Jones

> *The ardent golfer would play Mount Everest if somebody put a flagstick on top.*
>
> -Pete Dye

At the Sleepy Hollow golf course, a foursome approached the 11th tee where the fairway runs along the edge of the course and adjoins a highway.

Forrester teed off and sliced the ball right over the fence. It hit the front tire of a bus and bounced back onto the green and into the cup for a hole-in-one.

"How on earth did you ever get it to bounce off that bus?" asked one of his astonished buddies.

"Well, first off," he replied, "you've got to know the bus schedule."

• • • •

Two duffers are downing a few at the nineteenth hole when one says to the other, "I'm taking my wife to the Holy Land to walk where the saints once walked."

The second duffer says, "Oh, you're taking her to Jerusalem?"

"Jerusalem. Heck no. I'm taking her to St. Andrews."

Sometimes You Just Can't Win

In 1982, John Murphy went out to play a quiet round of golf by himself in Raleigh, North Carolina. To his amazement he aced the fifth hole but because he was alone, it wasn't official. After the game, Murphy led the assistant greenskeeper back to the fifth hole, teed up and repeated the hole-in-one. Sadly, as it wasn't scored during an official round, that one didn't count either.

"The shortest distance between any two points on a golf course is a straight line that passes directly through the center of a very large tree." -Confucius

• •

"Lost: Golfing husband and dog- last seen at Ratliff Ranch Golf Links. Reward for dog." -Newspaper ad put in by a golfing widow from Midland, Texas, apparently fed up with her husband's love for the game

Playing with your spouse on the golf course runs almost as great a marital risk as getting caught with someone else's anywhere else.

-Peter Andrews

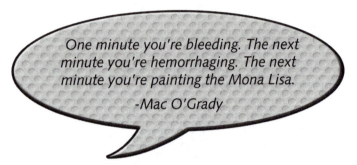

One minute you're bleeding. The next minute you're hemorrhaging. The next minute you're painting the Mona Lisa.

-Mac O'Grady

Walter Diets scored his first hole-in-one on a course near Los Angeles in 1987. What makes it so unusual is that he was blind. Walter had played the course for years when he could see, but it wasn't until his first time out without vision that he shot an ace.

•

Amateur Jim Whelehan of Rochester, NY, was playing an 18-hole round in 1992 when he shot a hole-in-one on the fourth hole of the Heather Glen Golf Links in Myrtle Beach, SC. Thrilled by his feat, he decided to play a second round and later that day, same ball, same hole, same result- he aced it once again.

•

During World War II, British golfers were asked to pick up bomb and shell fragments off the course to help the greenskeeper spare damage to the lawnmowers.

•

Despite losing an eye in World War I, Tommy Armour still won three major titles: the U.S. Open in 1927, the PGA Championship in 1930, and the British Open in 1931.

SENIOR CITIZENS

1. Who's the oldest golfer to win a Major?

2. What do the following have in common: Old Tom Morris, Hale Irwin, Julius Boros and Jack Nicklaus? (Hint: Question number one should help you out.)

3. How old must you be to play on the Champions Tour?

4. Who was the first man to win both the U.S. Open and the Senior Open?

5. Who, in 1980, was the first winner of the U.S. Senior Open:

        a) Roberto DeVicenzo   b) Dave Stockton
        c) Miller Barber   d) Red Barber?

ANSWERS: 1.Julius Boros- He was 48 when he won the 1968 PGA Championship. 2.They are the oldest winners of each of the four Majors: respectively, the British Open, U.S. Open, PGA Championship and Masters. 3.50 4.Arnold Palmer- He won the second Senior Open. 5.A

> *I hit two fairways - well, maybe four,*
> *but only two I was aiming at.*
>
> *-John Daly*

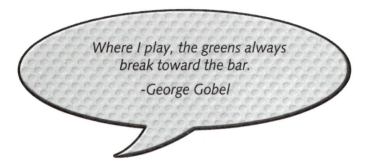

Where I play, the greens always break toward the bar.

-George Gobel

These Golfers Needed
Two Pairs of Socks...

...Because they got a hole in one. (Sorry, but we had to fit the world's oldest golf groaner in here somehow.)

53-year-old Sheila Drummond recorded a 144-yard hole-in-one at the Mahoning Valley Country Club, near Lehighton, Pennsylvania, in 2007. Mrs. Drummond is blind.

• •

Harold Stilson, from Boca Raton, Florida, became the oldest player ever to hit a hole-in-one when he aced the 16th hole at the Deerfield Country Club on May 16, 2001, at the age of 101.

• •

Dave Ragaini used a 3-wood at a 207 yard, par-3 hole at Wykagyl Country Club at New Rochelle, New York and hit a hole-in-one. Oh, yes - he was standing on his knees at the time!

On New Year's Eve in 1989 Jenny Ritchie celebrated with a hole-in-one at New Zealand's Wanganui Golf Club. The following day, same place, same story- another ace!

• •

The longest recorded hole-in-one by a woman occurred in 1949 when Marie Robie aced the 393- yard hole at Furnace Brook in Wollaston, MA.

• •

Tiger Woods was six years old when he hit his first hole in one. He has 18.

• •

Jack Nicklaus has 20 aces; his last came in a practice round when he was 63. Gary Player has 19, his last at the age of 70 and Arnold Palmer has 18. He was 74 when he made his last one.

• •

Three U.S. presidents have recorded aces: Dwight Eisenhower, Richard Nixon and Gerald Ford. Nixon said his hole in one at the Bel Air Country Club in 1961, was "the greatest thrill in my life."

My favorite shots are the practice swing and the conceded putt. The rest can never be mastered.

-Lord Robertson

> *One lesson you better learn if you want to be in politics is that you never go out on a golf course and beat the President.*
>
> *-President Lyndon B. Johnson*

"You're going out to play golf again?" sighed the golf widow.

"But Honey, I'm under doctor's orders," the husband replied as he stopped in the doorway.

"How dumb do you think I am?" the wife asked.

"Really Dear, it's true. At my last checkup he told me to get plenty of iron every day."

Ned and Mack were very competitive at golf and very closely matched. One day they decided on a "play it as it lies" round to break the deadlock.

The number one hole was a par 4 and both players drove it right down the middle, about 250 yards. They drove the golf cart up for the second shot and Ned hit a great shot to the green within 12 feet of the hole.

Mack, however sliced his over the trees and right onto the cart path of the adjoining hole.

"Well, I guess I get a free drop from the cart path," Mack said.

Ned pointed out that it was a strict "Play it as it lays" game and so he drove up to the green to finish and Mack drove to his ball over on the cart path.

Ned putted his ball in easily and looked up to see Mack taking wild practice swings which sent up showers of sparks. He chuckled at his opponent's misfortune until Mack took a perfect swing and sent the ball flying right into the cup. With that, Mack drove back to the green to pick up Ned.

"That was amazing!" Ned exclaimed. "A fantastic shot- and after all those sparks. What club did you use?"

Mack just smiled and said, "Your five iron."

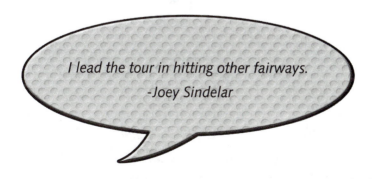

I lead the tour in hitting other fairways.
-Joey Sindelar

The actual distance a bad golfer is going to hit the ball with any club obviously depends on many factors, not the least of which is whether the ball was actually hit at all.

-Leslie Nielsen

HOME SWEET HOME

Match the golfers with their native country.

1. Inbee Park   a) Fiji

2. Ian Woosnam   b) England

3. Vijay Singh   c) South Africa

4. Ernie Els   d) South Korea

5. Ian Poulter   e) Wales

ANSWERS: 1.D 2.E 3.A 4.C 5.B

"I'll get up at five in the morning to do only two things: go to the bathroom and play golf."

–Former pro football quarterback Jim McMahon

TRIVIA

Harvey Penick's "Little Red Book" is the best selling sports book in history, with more than two million copies sold.

•

"National Lampoon" says: "If you want to take long walks, take long walks. If you want to hit things with a stick, hit things with a stick. But there's no excuse for combining the two and putting the results on TV."

•

The first golf instruction book printed was "The Golfer's Manual." Written by Henry B. Farnie in 1857, it discussed the mechanics of the swing and proper use of equipment.

•

In 1888, the St. Andrew's GC of Yonkers, N.Y., spent a total of $28.42 for the upkeep of the six-hole golf course.

•

The green jacket was introduced at the 1949 Masters. The first recipient was Sam Snead.

If every golfer in the world, male and female, were laid end to end, I for one, would leave them there.

-Mark Parkinson, President of the Anti-Golf Society

> *Probably I'm a hell of a lot more famous for being the guy who hit the golf ball on the moon than the first guy in space.*
>
> -Astronaut Alan Shepard

The Masters was the first major to switch from an 18-hole playoff to sudden death, making the change in 1976.

•

In 1457, golf was outlawed in Scotland because the lawmakers felt that time spent on the game would be better invested in archery practice to defend Scotland from the English. Guess they didn't realize most golfers could take somebody out faster with a golf ball than an arrow.

•

The 1965 U.S. Open was the first to be played in a four-day format of 18 holes each day. Before that, golfers played 18 holes the first two days and a 36-hole final day.

•

In 1946, Byron Nelson was in the hunt for his second U.S. Open title when his caddy lost his balance and kicked Nelson's ball. That cost Nelson a penalty stroke which would come back to haunt him. He eventually lost the title in a three-way playoff.

OF COURSE

1. Flooded fairways caused officials to cancel what 1996 PGA Tour event?

2. Which country has the most golf courses in the world?

3. What state has the most golf courses in the U.S.?

4. The eighteenth tee at what course is called "Nicklaus tee"?

5. Which golf course, played at 7,674 yards, is the longest in major championship history?

ANSWERS: 1.The AT&T Pebble Beach National Pro-Am 2.The United States has, far and away, the most- almost half of the world's estimated 35,000 golf courses. 3.Florida 4.Harbour Town, home of the Heritage Golf Classic on Hilton Head Island in South Carolina... It was so nicknamed because of the 250 yard drive it would take to reach a peninsula area of the fairway. Nicklaus would routinely take just one drive to reach it. 5.Hazeltine in Chaska, Minnesota, which hosted the 2009 PGA won by Y.E. Yang

The sand was heavier than I thought and it only took me four swings to figure it out.

-Johnny Miller

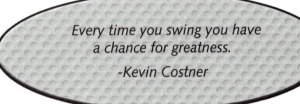

*Every time you swing you have
a chance for greatness.*
-Kevin Costner

POTUS declares golf
'great exercise' but...

U.S. President Ulysses S. Grant was of Scottish ancestry and in the 1870s, among his travels following his presidency, was a trip to the birthplace of golf. While in Scotland, Grant was shown a "demonstration" of this new game. Unfortunately, the person designated to showcase the game for the former president was a horrible hacker. After placing the ball on the tee, the golfer feebly attempted to meet the ball numerous times but wound up hitting huge divots again and again. After watching this for a while, Grant observed, "The game appears to be great exercise. But tell me, what is the purpose of the little white ball?"

Practice Makes Perfect

When rain washed out the first two rounds of the 1983 Hong Kong Open, Greg Norman practiced by driving golf balls out the open window of his hotel room into the harbor. He won the tourney.

Higgins was frantic and called his doctor. "Doc, it's Higgins. I've got an emergency. My baby just swallowed my golf tees!"

"I'll be right there!" exclaimed the doctor.

"But what do I do in the meantime?" cried Higgins.

"Practice your putting."

• • • •

Here's one from the star of "Caddyshack"- the man who got no respect –Rodney Dangerfield:

Every time my wife takes the car there's trouble. The other day she came home, there were 100 dents in the car. She said she took a shortcut through the driving range.

*My game is impossible to help.
Ben Hogan said every time he gave me a
lesson it added two shots to his game.*

-Phil Harris, comedian

> *I'll take a two-shot penalty, but I'll be damned if I'm going to play the ball where it lies.*
>
> *-Elaine Johnson, after her shot bounced off a tree and into her bra*

Gus was keeping score and asked Wilbur what he shot as they finished the sixth hole.

"A 14," said Wilbur.

"What- a 14?" said Gus incredulously. "How did you ever manage a 14 on a par-3?

"I sank a 35-foot putt."

• • • •

A coroner examined the corpse of the golfer's wife, then began interrogating the husband. "Is that your Top-Flite that's embedded in the temple of the deceased."

"Yes, it is," the golfer admits.

"And why is there a second Top-Flite embedded in her back?"

The golfer answers, "The temple shot was my mulligan."

FIRST THINGS FIRST

1. What is Tiger Woods' first name?

2. In 1979, who became the first player known to score lower than his age, shooting a 67 at the Quad Cities Open at the age of 66?

3. In 2013, Inbee Park put up "Ruthian" numbers remindful of the golfer who was the first female to win the first three women's majors of a season, in 1950. Who was she?

4. Who was the first African American to play at the Masters?

5. Who was the first player to win $5 million in a year? (Hint: The year was 1988.)

ANSWERS: 1.Eldrick 2.Sam Snead 3."Babe" Zaharias 4.Lee Elder, in 1975 5.Jack Nicklaus

My putter will not be flying first-class home with me.

-Nick Faldo

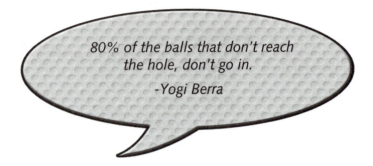

80% of the balls that don't reach the hole, don't go in.

-Yogi Berra

Man dies on golf course, friends play through

Believe it or not, the headline you just read was a real one, albeit a real old one, from an Associated Press release. Officials at a Winter Haven, Florida, golf course covered the golfer's body with a sheet "right where he died, on the 16th green. The body stayed there two hours, while friends and neighbors played through." "It was a real shock to all of us, but there was nothing we could do," said one of the golfers. "We all thought to ourselves, 'Gee, that's a good way to go.' He didn't suffer."

"To really lose weight playing golf...Go to any Mexican golf course, stop at every hole and drink water. Within a week you'll be down to your desired weight."

–Comedian Buddy Hackett

TRIVIA

The first golf magazine, "Golf: A Weekly Record of 'Ye Royal and Ancient' Game," appeared in Great Britain in 1890.

•

On a hot summer day at the 1986 Anheuser Busch Golf Classic, Bill Kratzert managed to lose three balls during play and had to withdraw from the event because he ran out of them. His caddie, trying to lighten the golf bag, didn't bring any extra ones!

•

"Do you believe in miracles?!" That famous line made by Al Michaels to describe the 1980 U.S. Olympic hockey team's win over the Soviet Union is used by the sportscaster to this day. Michaels admits, "It's usually on the golf course after a long birdie putt."

•

In 1977, Al Geiberger became the first golfer to shoot a round of 59 (at the Memphis Classic which he won). The only videotape of Geiberger's round was destroyed in a fire.

> *Belly dancers would make great golfers.*
> *They never move their heads.*
> -Phil Rodgers

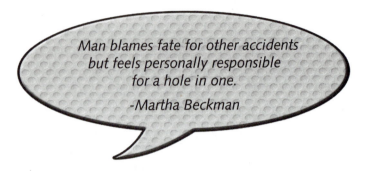

Man blames fate for other accidents
but feels personally responsible
for a hole in one.
-Martha Beckman

A MAN FOR ALL SEASONS

1. An avid amateur golfer, this tennis player was buried with his five-iron following his death in 1994.

2. Do you know the only man to play in both a World Series and a Masters tournament?

3. Who's the only one to win an Academy Award and make a hole-in-one on the 16th hole at Cypress Point?

4. Who was a teammate of baseball Hall of Famer Roberto Clemente on a Class A minor league team in Puerto Rico in 1953?

5. Baseball's all-time career batting leader was a member of Augusta National. Name him.

ANSWERS 1.Vitas Gerulaitis 2.Sam Byrd, who played in the 1931 Fall Classic for the Yankees and finished in the top five in both the 1941 and 1942 Masters 3.Bing Crosby, who won an Oscar for Going My Way in 1944 and, in 1948, aced one of the toughest par 3s in golf 4.Chi Chi Rodriguez 5.Ty Cobb

Wife: I have some bad news and some worse news.

Hubby: What's the bad news?

Wife: I ran over your clubs.

Hubby: Geez! What's the worse news?

Wife: They were on the front porch.

• • • •

While attending a conference in deepest, darkest Africa, a businessman found himself with some spare time. Since he had played golf on three other continents, he wanted to add Africa to his lifetime list. Finding the local golf course at the edge of the jungle, he asked the pro if he could get on.

"Of course," said the pro. "What's your handicap?"

The businessman was always a bit sensitive in that area and decided to drop it from 18 to 16 but was puzzled as to why they even asked.

> I've thrown clubs. I launched my 7-iron and managed to get it stuck in a tree. All my buddies were laughing because they know how competitive I am. They love torturing me in the only sport I can't beat them.
> -Michael Phelps

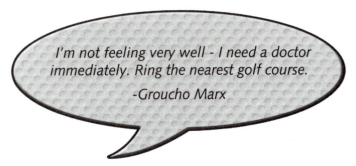

I'm not feeling very well - I need a doctor immediately. Ring the nearest golf course.

-Groucho Marx

"It's very important that we know," said the pro, who then called a caddy. "This gentleman's handicap is a 16," he told the caddy. He then bid the businessman good luck and went on his way.

The businessman was surprised at the constant references to his handicap as well as the fact that the caddy carried a large rifle but he decided not to ask any questions.

On the first hole the caddy advised him that it was important to avoid the trees to the right. Naturally, the businessman hit directly into the trees and while he was looking for his ball, he heard a shot whizz by over his head and a huge snake fell dead at his feet.

"Black Mamba," the caddy said. "Deadliest snake in Africa."

On the next hole, the caddy cautioned him to stay clear of the brush on the left and of course, the businessman hit right into it. While retrieving the ball, he felt the hot breath of a roaring lion on his neck just before a shot rang out nicking the lion's ear and scaring it off.

"Saved your life again," the caddy said." Now whatever you do on this next hole, stay away from the lake."

Sure enough, on the next hole, the businessman missed the green and the ball rolled down to the edge of the lake. As the businessman was preparing to swing, a huge crocodile lunged from the water and snapped off his leg below the knee.

As he lay there in horrific pain, trying to fashion a tourniquet from his belt, the businessman cried out "Why didn't you shoot him?"

And the caddy replied quite matter-of-factly, "Sorry sir, this is the 17th handicap hole, you don't get a shot here."

And that golfers, is why you should never, ever lie about your handicap.

It takes Latinos nine hours to play golf. Four hours for eighteen holes, and five hours to do the lawn.

-George Lopez

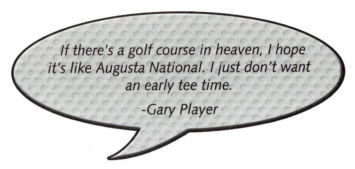

If there's a golf course in heaven, I hope it's like Augusta National. I just don't want an early tee time.

-Gary Player

Up until 1982, golfers were assigned local caddies for the Masters and were not allowed to bring their own.

•

The largest collection of golf books in the world belongs to the USGA Museum and Library, which has a collection of golf magazines dating back to 1880.

•

The average age of a PGA Tour professional is 35.

•

At Uganda's Jinja Golf Course, you must let elephants play through- they have the right of way.

•

Former president George W. Bush and future wife Laura spent their first date at a miniature golf course.

•

Winless in 18 years on the PGA Tour, Gary McCord had "NO WINS" inscribed on his vanity license plate. When he finally won on the Hogan Tour in 1991, McCord added an asterisk to the plate.

How Could He Miss?
There are Holes in Every Direction!

Alan Shepard became the first extraterrestrial golfer when he retrieved his smuggled 6-iron and package of balls from Apollo XIV in February, 1971 and took some practice shots on the moon. Even his poorest shot in the low gravity, airless environment of the lunar surface soared over 400 yards. As Shepard remarked with some satisfaction, "Not bad for a 6-iron!"

• • • •

Maybe you've heard about the cold weather golfer who, when on the green, would take a swig from his hip flask to ward off the frigid temperatures. It became known as the shot putt.

How is a wedding ring like a bag of golf clubs?
They are both instruments of eternal servitude.

I had a wonderful experience on the golf course today. I had a hole in nothing. Missed the ball and sank the divot.

-Don Adams

> *I like golf because when somebody tells
> the gallery to be quiet, they get quiet.
> Try that in baseball and they get louder.*
>
> -Mark McGwire

TROPHY CASE

1. The winner of what tournament receives the Francis D. Ouimet Memorial Trophy?

2. What kind of object is the British Open trophy?

3. The Masters trophy is a replica of what landmark?

4. The Sam Snead Cup is presented to the winner of what Tour stop?

5. Do you know the golfer who made a cameo appearance in a driving-range scene in the movie "Tin Cup"?

ANSWERS: 1.The U.S. Senior Open 2.A claret jug 3.The clubhouse at Augusta National 4.The Greater Greensboro Chrysler Classic 5.Johnny Miller

Negotiations were at a standstill between Big Joey Gabone, representing the union, and Morris Brathwaite, representing management. Braithwaite was accusing union members of abusing their contract's sick leave provisions. Gabone categorically denied it.

The next morning, Brathwaite showed up at the talks waving the local newspaper. "Here, look at the sports page," said Brathwaite, "This photo of a golfer under the headline 'Local man breaks club record.' That man is a union member and he called in sick yesterday."

The room fell silent for a few moments and Brathwaite felt quite self-satisfied until Gabone piped up with, "Unbelievable!"

"Oh you can believe it," crowed Brathwaite, "Pictures don't lie."

"I know," said Gabone."Imagine how well this guy would have played if he hadn't been sick."

Hell, I don't need to know where the green is. Where is the golf course?

-Babe Ruth, playing Pine Valley

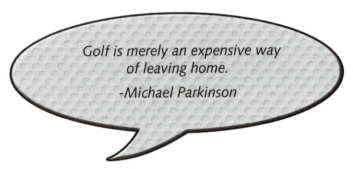

Golf is merely an expensive way of leaving home.

-Michael Parkinson

THE "A" LIST

Each of the following answers begin with the letter "A."

1. It's a hole shot that's three less strokes than par.

2. David Graham became the first _____ to win the U.S. Open.

3. What state has the fewest golf courses in America?

4. What is the ASGCA?

5. What woman comes first on the World Golf Hall of Fame alphabetical list?

ANSWERS: 1.Albatross 2.Australian 3.Alaska 4.American Society of Golf Course Architects 5.Amy Alcott

In a 10-second scene from the golf flick "Tin Cup," Kevin Costner hits a shot that banks off a portable toilet and onto the green, rolling right up to the camera lens. It required 86 takes and nearly the whole day to shoot it.

TRIVIA

JoAnn Washam is the only golfer to ace two holes in the same LPGA tournament. Washam did it in the second and final rounds of the 1979 Women's Kemper Open.

•

In 1899, golfers at the Atlantic City (N.J.) CC came up with the word "birdie" when George Crump put his second shot inches from the hole on a par four after his ball hit a bird in flight.

•

Way back when, this sports headline appeared in the "St. Louis Post-Dispatch": "Shot Off Woman's Leg Helps Nicklaus to 66."

•

Lingo of the Links: A "toilet flusher" is a putt that swirls around the rim of the hole.

•

Tee off at the "Fra Mauro Country Club" and you'll literally be hitting moon shots. That's the name of the lunar landing spot where Alan Shepard played golf.

> I've heard people say putting is 50% technique and 50% mental. I really believe it is 50% technique and 90% positive thinking. See, but that adds up to 140%, which is why nobody is 100% sure how to putt.
>
> -Chi Chi Rodriguez

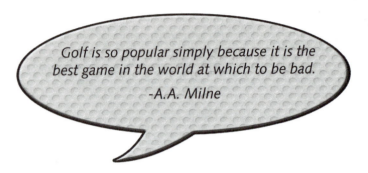

Golf is so popular simply because it is the best game in the world at which to be bad.

-A.A. Milne

Two psychologically fragile fellows are avid duffers who, coincidentally, have the same shrink who's prescribed the exact same treatment for them- a game of golf using an imaginary ball to reduce stress.

The two are paired together and tee off with their imaginary balls. Both of them hit magnificent imaginary drives down the middle of the fairway and wind up birdying the first hole. This continues throughout the round, a birdie here, an eagle there for each of them. It's become quite competitive, actually.

Finally, they reach the 18th hole dead even. Both of them hit tee shots that have their imaginary balls land on the green. The first guy lines up his "46-foot" putt and sinks the imaginary ball. He says to his playing partner, "Let's see what you can do now. The best you can hope for is a tie."

"I don't think so," his partner says matter of factly. "You just used my ball."

Sheldon's tee shot resulted in a horrible slice that flew over into the next fairway, conking a bystander in the head and knocking him cold. By the time he and his partner, Wally, arrived, the man was lying unconscious on the ground with the ball between his feet.

"What should I do?" Sheldon blurted out in a panic.

"Don't touch him," said Wally. "If we leave him here, he becomes an immovable obstruction and you can drop the ball two club lengths away."

Expensive Trip

At the 1988 Canadian Open, Dave Bally had an easy putt but as he approached his ball, he tripped, sending his putter flying into the ball and knocking it off the green into a nearby pond. He wound up with a triple bogey on the par three hole.

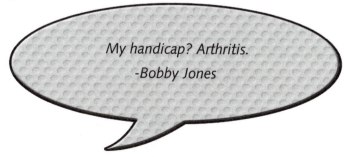

My handicap? Arthritis.

-Bobby Jones

> *A driving range is the place where golfers go to get all the good shots out of their system.*
>
> -Henry Beard

A priest, a doctor and a lawyer were becoming frustrated with the slow play of the foursome ahead of them. "What's with these guys," the lawyer grumbled. "We've been waiting to tee off at least 15 minutes."

"Here comes the greenskeeper," said the priest. "Let's have a word with him."

When confronted, the greenskeeper advised them that the slow-playing group were firefighters and that, sadly, they all lost their sight while saving the clubhouse from a fire a year ago. In gratitude, the club allowed them to play for free anytime.

The priest expressed his concern and said he'd keep them in his prayers while the doctor volunteered to contact an ophthalmologist buddy to see if there was anything he could do for them.

The lawyer said, "Why can't these guys play at night?"

ONE FOR THE AGES

1. In 2009, what 59-year-old finished second in a four hole playoff in the Open Championship at Turnberry?

2. What 76-year-old competed in his last British Open in 1896?

3. Name the 46-year-old who won the 1986 Masters.

4. When be turned 50 and became eligible for the PGA Senior Tour, he said, "I went to bed on September 4, 1992, and I was old and washed up. I woke up a rookie. What could be better?" Who said it?

5. Who was the oldest player ever to finish in the top 10 at the Masters?

ANSWERS: 1.Tom Watson (Stewart Cink was the winner.) 2.Old Tom Morris Sr. 3.Jack Nicklaus 4.Ray Floyd 5.Jack Nicklaus, when he tied for sixth in 1998 at the age of 58 years, two months, and 21 days

I don't know of any game that makes you so ashamed of your profanity. It is a game full of moments of self-abasement, with only a few moments of self-exaltation.

-President William Howard Taft

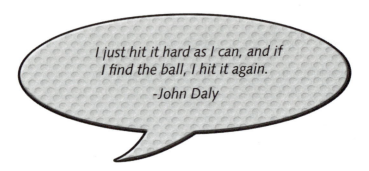

*I just hit it hard as I can, and if
I find the ball, I hit it again.*

-John Daly

In 2006, 12-year old Blake Hadden from North Augusta, South Carolina, recorded two holes-in-one in the 11-12 age group at the Future Masters. Hadden aced the 83-yard number 5 hole and the 140-yard number 11 hole at the Dothan Country Club in Alabama.

•

At the Kampala Golf Club in Uganda you're allowed free relief from hippopotamus footprints. Golfers are also warned to avoid water hazards on ten of the eighteen holes where there's a danger of crocodiles.

•

Only one golfer has shot two holes-in-one in British Open competition. Charles Ward aced the eighth at St. Andrews in 1946 and, two years later, shot a hole-in-one on the 13th at Muirfield.

•

Identical twins John and Desmond Rosser not only walk alike and talk alike, they even ace alike. The pair scored holes-in-one in consecutive rounds at New Zealand's Auckland Golf Club.

Albert had a bad day of golf- a really bad day. As he was walking through the parking lot on his way out, he was stopped by a policeman. "Excuse me sir, did you tee off on the 17th hole about a half hour ago?"

"Why yes, yes I did," Albert answered.

"And you hooked your ball over the trees and off the course?"

"I did," Albert answered.

The policeman continued, "Then it was your ball which went through the windshield of a station wagon causing it to stop suddenly and cause a chain reaction collision involving 8 cars. This resulted in a truck jack-knifing and blocking the road so that a fire engine couldn't get through, causing an apartment building to burn to the ground. So... What do you intend to do about it?"

Albert shook his head sadly and said, "The only thing I can do Officer. I've got to close my stance a bit, tighten my grip and lower my right thumb."

The first time Bob Gibson ever let himself get talked into a celebrity golf tournament, he shot a score of 115. It was his own fault. He counted all his strokes.

-Bob Uecker

> *Golf, like measles, should be caught young, for, if postponed to riper years, the results may be serious.*
>
> -P.G. Wodehouse

KEEPING IT SIMPLE

The following questions can be answered with a simple "yes" or "no."

1. Was miniature golf originally called "Tom Thumb Golf?"

2. Did Lee Trevino ever win the Masters?

3. Is former Secretary of State Condoleezza Rice a member of Augusta?

4. Was Greg Norman married to former tennis star Chris Evert?

5. Is a golf hole 5 inches in diameter?

ANSWERS: 1.Yes 2.No 3.Yes 4.Yes (briefly, from 2008-09) 5.No (Regulations call for it to be 4.25" wide.)

Jack Goes Clubbing

In a fit of road rage, Jack Nicholson once teed off on another driver's car with a golf club because he was cut off in traffic. He later said he was "out of his mind," but admitted he was rational enough to do the bashing with his 2-iron, which he never used on the links.

• • • •

The only blonde golf joke in the book:

A blonde goes into the pro shop and asks the manager, "Do you have any green golf balls?"

"No, we don't carry any green golf balls."

The blonde says, "Why not?"

The manager responds, "The question should be more like 'Why would we?"

"Isn't it obvious?" the blonde says with a smirk. "They're easier to find in the sand trap."

Golf is more fun than walking naked in a strange place, but not much.
-Buddy Hackett

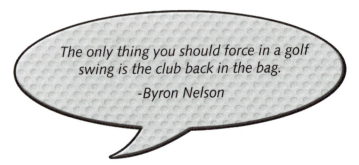

The only thing you should force in a golf swing is the club back in the bag.

-Byron Nelson

McMurphy's Laws

We all know Murphy's Law but only golfers can truly appreciate "McMurphy's Laws of the Links."

1. No matter how bad your last shot was, the worst is yet to come. This law extends far beyond the 18th hold to the course of a tournament, and ultimately, an entire lifetime.

2. Your best round of golf will be immediately followed by your worst round ever. The probability of the latter increases in direct proportion with the number of people you tell about the former.

3. Brand new golf balls are irresistibly attracted to water. The more expensive the ball, the greater the attraction.

4. "Nice lag" can be translated to "lousy putt." By the same token, "tough break" translates to "I can't believe you missed that last one, bonehead."

5. Palm trees eat golf balls.

6. Sand is alive. It's an evil, malevolent presence which exists solely to make golfers' lives miserable. Sand is Demon Dust.

7. Golf balls never bounce off trees back into play. If one ever does happen to, you can bet the devil will be teeing off in six inches of snow.

8. There is a point on every golf course that is the absolute furthest from the clubhouse. You'll know you are there when your cart runs out of juice.

9. The person you would most hate to lose to will always be the one who beats you.

10. Golf should be sworn off at least three times a month...and sworn at the rest of the time.

• • • •

Golf is a lot like taxes. You drive hard to get to the green and you wind up in the hole.

My putting is so bad I could putt it off a tabletop and leave it short, halfway down a leg.

-J.C. Snead

> *Around the clubhouse they'll tell you that even God has to practice his putting. In fact, even Nicklaus does.*
>
> *-Jim Murray*

A.K.A.

1. What's the slang term for the score of an 8 on a hole?

2. During the presidency of Bill Clinton, what were his "do-overs" on the course called?

3. What slang term refers to the fringe around the green?

4. What are knickers worn by golfers known as?

5. A banana ball is a slang term that can be used to described what type of shot?

ANSWERS: 1.Snowman 2.Billigans 3.Frog Hair 4.Plus-fours 5.A slice

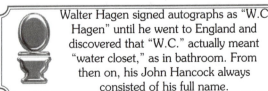

Walter Hagen signed autographs as "W.C. Hagen" until he went to England and discovered that "W.C." actually meant "water closet," as in bathroom. From then on, his John Hancock always consisted of his full name.

TRIVIA

At his 50th wedding anniversary party held at the local country club, Ralph was asked the secret of his long marriage. He stood up before his assembled crowd of friends and relatives and shared his marital philosophy.

"Gertrude and I have made it a practice throughout our long marriage to play golf and then go out for two romantic, candlelit dinners a week - right here at this country club. Unfailingly, twice a week, we come here and enjoy the delicious food and soft music. We soak up the ambiance of this fine establishment and sip a vintage wine. She goes Thursdays and I go Fridays."

• • • •

Morty and Fred were teeing off early one summer's day when the usual tranquility of the golf course was shattered by the siren of an ambulance racing to the maternity hospital atop a nearby hill.

"Somebody's getting a big surprise today," said Morty.

"I'll say," replied Fred as he lined up his putt. "When I left this morning, my wife's contractions were still at least an hour apart."

> *That little white ball won't move until you hit it, and there's nothing you can do after it has gone.*
> *-Babe Zaharias*

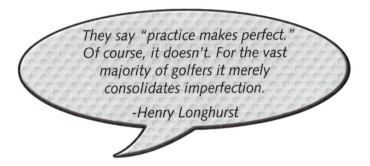

They say "practice makes perfect." Of course, it doesn't. For the vast majority of golfers it merely consolidates imperfection.

-Henry Longhurst

AGAINST THE ODDS

1. In 1949, he had a near fatal car crash with a bus. A year later, he won the U.S. Open. Name him.

2. According to "Golf Digest," the odds of doing this twice in a single round of golf are 67 million to one.

3. In 1999, Paul Lawrie was 10 strokes down and made the biggest final round comeback in PGA history when he won what major?

4. In 1913, what 20-year-old stunned Harry Vardon and Ted Ray in a playoff to become the first amateur winner of the U.S. Open?

5. Trailing by seven strokes on the final day, who shot a record-tying 64 to win his third green jacket at Augusta in 1978?

ANSWERS: 1.Ben Hogan 2.Making a hole in one 3.The British Open 4.Francis Ouimet 5.Gary Player

On a goodwill tour of South America, Sam Snead was about to hit a bunker shot when an ostrich attacked him. The bird was apparently interested in Snead's trademark straw hat. When Snead put up his hand to protect his face, the ostrich bit it. Slammin' Sammy was unable to play golf for two weeks.

•

Lloyd Mangrum lost the 1950 U.S. Open championship to Ben Hogan all because of a gnat. As he was about to putt, the fly landed on Mangrum's ball, and without thinking, he picked up the ball to swat away the gnat. For this he earned a 2-stroke penalty and ultimately lost the tournament to Hogan in a playoff.

•

That was the way it was: Until 1870 a player teed off for the next hole from the green of the preceding hole.

•

In 1922, Walter Hagen became the first golf professional to manufacture golf clubs under his own name.

I used to play golf with a guy who cheated so badly that he once had a hole-in-one and wrote down zero on the scorecard.

-Bobby Brue

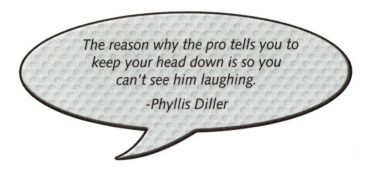

The reason why the pro tells you to keep your head down is so you can't see him laughing.

-Phyllis Diller

Bumper Snickers

• GOLFERS EXPRESS THEMSELVES TO A TEE

• GOLF COURSES ARE OFTEN GROUNDS FOR DIVORCE

• I BRAKE FOR ANIMALS BUT SINK BIRDIES

• MY OTHER CAR IS A GOLF CART

• GOLF SEPARATES THE MEN FROM THE POISE

• CAUTION: GOLFER AT WHEEL- DRIVER IN TRUNK

• MAY THE COURSE BE WITH YOU

• IF YOU THINK I'M A LOUSY DRIVER, YOU SHOULD SEE ME PUTT

• I'D RATHER BE DRIVING MY GOLF BALL

A guy goes to the doctor for a checkup. Afterwards, the doctors says, "I've got good news and bad news."

The guy says, "Give me the bad news first, Doc."

"You've got an incurable disease and probably won't live more than a year."

"Geez, what could possibly be the good news?"

"I broke 80 yesterday."

• • • •

Barrington: I say, did you hear what happened to Rockingham?

Hyde-White: No, I'm afraid I haven't.

Barrington: He was awakened in the middle of the night by a burglar and beat the miscreant into submission with a five-iron.

Hyde-White: Do tell. How many strokes?

> *How did I four-putt? I missed the hole. I missed the hole. I missed the hole. I made it.*
>
> *-Fuzzy Zoeller*

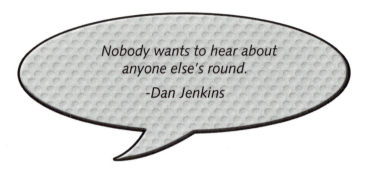

Nobody wants to hear about anyone else's round.

-Dan Jenkins

The Top Ten Ways To Tell You're A Golf Widow

10. When hubby refers to his "better half", he's talking about the back nine.

9. If you ever had to skip town after a golf bet went sour

8. He forgets your anniversary but annually marks the observance of the day he first played at Pebble Beach.

7. If you've ever had to put the 19th Hole on speed-dial

6. The only dimples he appreciates any more are on golf balls.

5. He tells you that you deserve a second honeymoon and then leaves you on a golf vacation.

4. If going out as a foursome never includes you

3. His idea of renewing his vows is telling you exactly what he yelled after missing that two-foot putt.

2. You don't need the Weather Channel. If he's home, it's raining.

And the NUMBER ONE way to tell if you're a golf widow…

When he says he's going out to "play a round," you almost wish he would.

Out on a Limb

In 1993, Germany's Bernhard Langer lodged a ball twenty feet up in a tree while playing in a tournament in England. Langer climbed the tree and knocked the ball out. Afterwards, when asked what club he had used, Langer responded, "a tree iron, of course."

Columbus went around the world in 1492. That isn't a lot of strokes when you consider the course.

-Lee Trevino

> *One time I was complaining that my shot was going to wind up in the water. So my friend told me that I should think positive. I told him okay, I was positive my shot was going to wind up in the water.*
> *-Yogi Berra*

A politician died and, as might be expected, he went straight to Hell. As Satan was showing him around the place, he noticed a beautiful golf course that would put Augusta to shame. Being a lifelong golf fanatic, he was thrilled. Striding into the pro shop, he spotted a sign that read, "Only The Finest Equipment And All Absolutely Free – Help Yourself."

Having selected a fantastic set of matched clubs and a first class golf bag, he next needed a caddy. The caddy shack was filled with gorgeous women who were movie stars in life. He chose Marilyn Monroe, who was wearing a teddy. He couldn't wait to begin his dream game! As he stepped up to the tee, he reached into the ball pocket and found it empty. He looked up to see Satan grinning from ear to ear.

"Don't bother going back to the pro shop. There aren't any balls anywhere – you see, that's the Hell of it."

SECOND GUESSING

1. In 2000, who became the first man to finish second in three consecutive majors?

2. What 1959 PGA Championship winner finished second in the U.S. Open in both 1959 and '69?

3. Who failed to become the second-youngest Masters winner in 2011 after shooting the worst final round in the tournament's history by a 54-hole leader?

4. What women's golf legend is second all-time in both LPGA Tour wins and major titles?

5. After capturing the British Open in 2013, the only major he hasn't won is the U.S. Open- an event in which he has finished second a record six times. Name him.

ANSWERS: 1.Ernie Els 2.Bob Rosburg 3.Rory McIlroy 4.Mickey Wright 5.Phil Mickelson

The Senior Tour is like a class reunion.
It's the same as it was thirty years ago.
We tell the same dirty jokes only
they're funnier now.

-Bob Toski

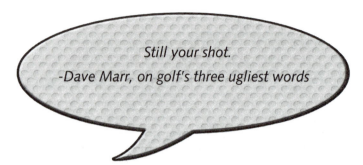

Still your shot.
-Dave Marr, on golf's three ugliest words

TAKE YOUR PICK

In which of the four major championships...

1. ...was match play used until 1958?

2. ...is the final round traditionally played on Father's Day?

3. ..is there a four-hole playoff format?

4. ...does the location remain the same from year to year?

5. ...does "glory's last shot" occur?

ANSWERS: 1.PGA Championship 2.U.S. Open 3.British Open
4.The Masters 5.PGA Championship

When golfer Johnny Pott was introduced
at the Los Angeles Open in the 1960s,
the announcer committed this blooper:
"Now on the pot, Johnny Tee!"

Miniature Golf

...One-liners on the links

Golf is the most popular way of beating around the bush.

A caddie is a lie-detector.

Golf is nature's way of telling you, "This is what life looks like from behind a tree."

You can judge a man by the golf score he keeps.

Golf is a very popular game- the only sport that can convert a duck pond into a water hazard.

The one advantage bowling has over golf is that you very rarely lose the ball.

Whoever said golf was fun either has never played golf or has never had any fun.

I owe a lot to my parents, especially my mother and father.

-Greg Norman

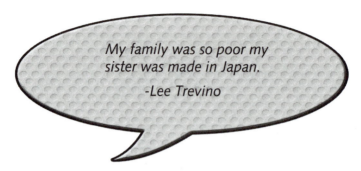

My family was so poor my sister was made in Japan.

-Lee Trevino

GETTING SOME COLOR

1. What color jacket does the winner of the Arnold Palmer Invitational receive?

2. In 1982, Wayne Levi became the first player to win on the PGA Tour with a ball that wasn't white. What color ball did he use to win the Hawaiian Open?

3. Who is known as the "Black Knight"?

4. This golfer received two Purple Hearts for his efforts during the Battle of the Bulge and, after World War II, came home and won the 1946 U.S. Open. Do you know him?

5. In 2006, Corey Pavin set a PGA Tour scoring record for nine holes when he shot a 26 on the front nine in the U.S. Bank Championship on this colorful course.

ANSWERS: 1.Navy blue 2.Orange 3.Gary Player 4.Lloyd Mangrum 5.Brown Deer Park

By the numbers: Arnold Palmer took part in fifty Masters tournaments. During that time it was calculated that he took 11,248 shots and played 2,718 holes measuring about 600 miles, which Palmer covered on foot.

•

Because of the wartime rubber shortage, golf balls were in scarce supply in 1945. Sam Snead, who said he was paying $100 a dozen for balls, won the Los Angeles Open while playing the entire tournament with one ball- it was given to him by Bing Crosby.

•

Golfers are always in for a seasonal treat at the Bjorkliden Golf Club in Sweden (150 miles north of the Arctic Circle). Reindeer serve as caddies on the course and there are some unique rules there such as:
"If a reindeer eats your ball, drop a new one where the incident occurred."

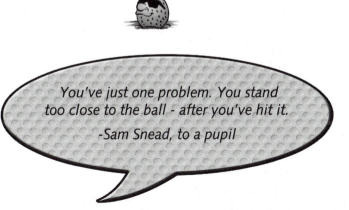

You've just one problem. You stand too close to the ball - after you've hit it.

-Sam Snead, to a pupil

> *If you call on God to improve the results of a shot while it is still in motion, you are using "an outside agency" and subject to appropriate penalties under the rules of golf.*
>
> *-Henry Longhurst*

Harvey the hacker had a burning ambition to play the 17th at Sawgrass and, just once, drive the ball out over the water and onto the green like the pros. A retired Floridian, he had played the hole many times, but his ball always fell short, into the water.

As a result, Harvey always used an old, beat up ball when he got to the 17th. On one such occasion, he teed up a used ball and said a silent prayer. All of the sudden, a voice from the heavens boomed, "Wait! Replace that old ball with a new one!"

Divine intervention! Harvey's dream was about to come true! He replaced the old ball with a new one and confidently stepped up to the tee. Again, that booming voice: "Wait. Take a practice swing first."

Harvey stepped back and took a practice swing. "Take another practice swing," boomed the heavenly voice.

Harvey took one more practice swing. Then, after a few moments of silence, he heard from upstairs again: "Never mind. Use the old ball."